TAKING IT ALL IN

BY

DAPHNE B MULIISA

ISBN 978-0-578-74856-6

Library of Congress Control Number 2020915935

Book cover design by Faith Nabaggala of Gala Image Consulting.

Layout by Generation Media.

Edited by Tiffanie James Parker, Ed. D of Phoenix Blue Academic Editing services.

Review by Daniel R.Ruhweza,PhD.

Printed in the United States of America

Dedication

To our beautiful girls- Crystal and Alyssa.

May your journey and testimony be an encouragement for another, to hold steadfast in the Lord and receive their breakthrough.

I thank God for trusting us with you. I hope this story will be an inspiration for others dealing with a special needs loved one and when you read this some day, you will remember how far God has brought you and How good He will always be to us as a family.

Table of Contents

Acknowledgments

First and foremost, I want to praise the Lord God Almighty who planted this seed into my heart and also gave me the grace to pursue it. When I got the revelation on January 2nd that happens to be my birthday, I was beyond terrified and confused by this 'strange' request from the Lord, to write this book. I am honored and humbled to have walked in obedience to God who has used me as His vessel.

Special thanks go to my father, the Honorable Justice Cheborion Barishaki for his leadership and guidance as I grew up. To my mother, Mrs. Lydia Barishaki, thank you for the endless love, encouragement, prayers and constant help with the kids during the summer breaks in this phase of life.

My family in love, the Tinkasimire's, please accept my warmest gratitude for the support and kindness you have shown me. I am extremely grateful to you, Mr. Francis Xavier Tinkasimire for spending the holidays with us and taking care of the children. Thank you Abwooli

Tinkasimire for your abundant love and support.

To my big sister Charlotte, words can't express my gratitude for the tireless prayers, fasting and daily encouragement you have given for the girls to receive their miracle.

To my siblings, Venasha, Sarah, Mercy, Siwa and Janet, and my brothers in law ProfessorTumuhairwe, Mr. Phillips and Dr. Cherop thank you for your constant checks on the girls and for the encouragement you have given Michael and I to trust the Lord as we raise these jewels from the Lord. I am forever grateful.

Special appreciation to my sister Joyce Chekwel who has stayed by our side and helped us raise the girls.

My best friend Sandra and husband Emmanuel, our precious Emmanuella and Peter Alan, may God forever bless you abundantly for holding our hands through this journey.

Our Word in Action Church. Pastors Mark and Tinah Mintah and the whole church family at Word In Action Church, these are your children. Thank you from the bottom of our hearts for everything.

Thanks also go to Pastor Fred Musasizi of Namuwongo Christ's center of Healing Ministries Kampala for your constant prayer and direction.

My supernatural Women family, you rock. You have been with us through it all and your love and support are what has helped me be better mother each day.

These acknowledgements would not be complete without mentioning my friends Mary, Anita, Lillian, Peninah, Ekua, Nabuduwa, Barbara, Sara, Brigitte, Stephanie, Lindsey, Jane, Kate, Richard, among others. Thank you so much for the love and kindness.

Finally, to my very wonderful husband Michael, my deepest gratitude goes to you. Thank you for being such a great sport, the best father the children could ever have and a team player for me even when somethings don't make sense, you always trust in the process and have always shown your support I love you and more, May God continue to be our strength and shield.

Enjoy the book.

Psalm 6:1-3

*O Lord, do not rebuke me in Your anger, Nor chasten
me in Your hot displeasure.
Have mercy on me, O Lord, for I am weak; O Lord,
heal me, for my bones are troubled.
My soul also is greatly troubled; But You, O Lord—
how long?*

CHAPTER ONE

THE DUST

It was a summer afternoon when I went for my usual prenatal checkup which actually happened to be my second to last. As I was nearing my due date, my doctor rushed me off to the hospital because I had developed pre-eclampsia, and I had to deliver our daughter as soon as possible. About five days later, we welcomed Crystal into the world. She was tiny, beautiful, and healthy. We left the hospital as first-time parents, excited and nervous at what life had in store for us. The first two months required a lot of adjusting to because she cried a lot. In the third month, she later adjusted, stopped crying, and slept throughout the night.

Towards the end of the third month, I discovered I was expecting our second child; I was nervous and concerned since we were just beginning to adjust to the new addition. We were also excited about the blessing. An additional blessing worth thanking God for is that, in this pregnancy, I did not struggle with morning sickness. I got dizzy spells occasionally in the afternoons, but they usually cleared up as soon as I laid down. I went for all my antenatal checkups, and at the beginning of the third trimester, I was told my baby was not growing anymore and that I needed to be monitored constantly for her growth. Every week, we would drive downtown to the hospital where I would be hooked up to monitors to record her growth patterns. During this time, we had also asked my mother to come over to help us. She agreed and started to prepare for the journey.

After about three weekly visits, the doctor determined that, indeed, our second born had stopped growing, and the only way to monitor everything was for me to give birth. We scheduled a C-section and beautiful Alyssa came into this world exactly one year and four days after Crystal. She was in the NICU for about three days, and my mother took good care of her along with the nurses and the doctors while I was trying to recover.

Life with our beautiful daughters was tedious and hectic in the beginning, but a joy, nonetheless. I was now a full-time mother who had decided to put work on pause and go back to school to pursue my master's degree. In between, we decided to take the girls back to my native land of Uganda to meet their grandparents, aunties, uncles, and cousins. The girls overall were doing well, learning how to crawl, walk, run, get their first teeth, and eat solids. My sister Joyce later came to visit, and she was such a big help; they loved her. She took care of them in every way you could imagine, and we were so grateful.

It was a beautiful day and I had my hands full between doing laundry, studying for an upcoming exam, and taking the girls for the usual routine checkup with the pediatrician. Michael came from work at about noon because the appointment I had set was for 1:15 pm. I got the girls dressed and ready, then off we went to the doctor. When we got there, it seemed quiet and empty—seemed like the front staff was not even there. There was a sign-in sheet, so I gave the girls to Michael and went on to sign in the girls. The lady at the front desk came in roughly ten minutes later, and the girls were called into the back to see the doctor shortly thereafter.

The nurse checked their weight and height and showed us a room to sit and wait for the doctor. Before she left, she handed us the age milestone forms to fill out.

It was quite a lot seeing that I was filling out information for two children. The doctor finally came in when I was almost done with the forms. He proceeded to check each girl vision, hearing and other routine with Michael's help.

At this point, I was done with the paperwork and I handed it over to the doctor. He went over it very carefully, asked a few more questions then went on to recommend a second detailed eye and ear test for each girl, with a specialist. I was confused and asked the doctor if everything was okay. He stated the milestone delays were very worrying and he wanted to make sure there was nothing they had missed. He went on to ask us if we had heard of the term autism, to which we replied no, so he provided us with a detailed explanation. We left the office and got home to the usual 'feed and bathe the girls' routine then put them to bed.

Once it was dark and quiet, I researched this new condition the doctor had informed us about. I still didn't understand the magnitude of the issue at the time. The next day, Michael came home from work and I mentioned it to him in passing, and he brushed it off as normal baby delays.

Knowing myself and not liking the sinking feeling

in my stomach, I made the appointments for the detailed tests the following day. The dates they gave us were three months out so I called the doctor's office to let them know. The doctor stated that the waiting period was too long and that would have his nurse call to expedite the process.

We eventually got the appointments and went in for the checks up which turned out normal, but everything had to be sent over to the doctor for a final evaluation and interpretation of the results. We got a call a few days later to come in to see the doctor, and we did.

The doctor then told us that he wanted to first rule out the girls having a hearing and vision problem before eventually breaking the news that the girls were autistic. He provided a great deal of reading material, resources to use, and most importantly, he had us start early intervention through a speech therapist and recommended a formal diagnosis. At that point, the condition didn't appear to be very serious, so we were sad but still had hope. This was due to the fact that the first assumption had been wrong and the tests had turned out normal, so we figured that even the autism tests would not be necessary in the long run.

Still, as a mother, I was concerned. I started to look for some YouTube educational videos for the girls and I purchased some learning toys. I had read that stimulating the brain could help.

Psalms 119:143-149

Trouble and distress have come upon me, but your commands give me delight. Your statutes are always righteous; give me understanding that I may live. I call with all my heart; answer me, LORD, and I will obey your decrees. I call out to you; save me and I will keep your statutes. I rise before dawn and cry for help; I have put my hope in your word. My eyes stay open through the watches of the night, that I may meditate on your promises. Hear my voice in accordance with your love; preserve my life, LORD, according to your laws.

CHAPTER TWO

THE SUM OF PAIN.

I got a phone call a few days later and it was a speech therapist calling to see if she could come to spend time with the girls to determine how we could proceed. She had been directed by the doctor's office to contact us. We set up the appointment for the following day.

She came and spent time with the girls and recommended we have them officially diagnosed so she could start her work of helping them professionally.

We were directed to a facility for this testing and we made a 10 am appointment for the following week. The day came and we took the girls for their evaluations. We filled out lots of paperwork, mainly about their milestones and day to day activities. We were told they would carry out developmental screening and a comprehensive diagnostic evaluation.

The girls were then taken away to a room that looked like a toddler daycare classroom. We were told to leave so that the observations and tests could be done without any bias and interruptions.

This lasted for about an hour including breaks in between. We were then told that the information would be sent for further evaluation, and the results would be mailed to us. When we left, I was anxious but still thought everything was being blown out of proportion. I consoled myself thinking this was just a normal delay. I had read that it was rare to have two autistic children in one home, so that also gave me some consolation.

We got home and went about our business as we waited for the results. I embarked on teaching the girls using YouTube videos like Busy Beavers, Dave and Ava, and Peppa Pig.

We were also advised to enroll them in preschool for a few hours.

Hours became days, days became weeks, then one

day as I was standing outside waiting for the school bus to bring the girls home, the mailman came and handed me an envelope. From the address, I could tell this was it; the results were in.

I got the girls, fed and bathed them, then left them to play. Soon after, they fell asleep, I decided to use the quiet time to open the envelope.

I was very nervous and anxious all by myself in the room going through page by page. I don't remember reading anything past the first two pages, where it had been made clear the girls had not passed the tests and they were both on the spectrum for autism.

The pain hit very quickly and hard. I broke down and sobbed like I had lost everything. I had many questions for God. At this point, I called my best friend Sandra. I remember so well she was on a train from her day classes and clinicals, so she was exhausted. I could tell it in her voice, but I needed to channel everything out before my girls woke up from their nap.

She listened as I cried and cried since that was all I did. She then told me to get dressed and she would pick me up for us to go to church for the evening service.

I went to the service, a confused and distraught mess. I don't even remember what was preached that day; I just went through the emotions. Trying to digest all this that was too much to deal with.

Psalm 16:1-5

Preserve me, O God: for in thee do I put my trust.
O my soul, thou hast said unto the LORD, *Thou art*
my Lord: my goodness extendeth not to thee;
But to the saints that are in the earth, and to the
excellent, in whom is all my delight.
Their sorrows shall be multiplied that hasten after
another god: their drink offerings of blood will I not
offer, nor take up their names into my lips.
The LORD *is the portion of mine inheritance and of*
my cup: thou maintainest my lot.

CHAPTER THREE

THE UNCERTAINTY

The news slowly started to become the new normal. Some days were okay, while other days were full of questions. I spent my days either staring into space or googling everything having to do with autism. The more I read, the more confused I became and started to lose hope. I looked at our girls as they went by their day eating, sitting in corners, and sometimes, crying all day, as they couldn't express themselves if they wanted something or were in pain.

I also started to notice certain mannerisms that I just thought were normal before. Our younger one, Alyssa, would line up her toys and shoes in such a straight-line. She was obsessed with closing doors, and she was such a picky eater. She didn't like most of the foods other children liked—no nuggets, no chicken, no meats, and fish. Our older child, Crystal, would cry all day—literally. She had a problem with crowds and very loud noises. These were all things we never really paid attention to before.

Potty training was a total nightmare; we kept trying for each one, but we were not very persistent because we now knew it would take time and that we were no longer using the regular milestones.

I wondered how God could bless us then take away. In my mind, that is what it seemed like. I looked at my girls every day, and the future was bleak. I wondered if they would ever be able to potty train fully, if they would ever feed themselves, and if they would learn to be independent. I thought of the bullies of this world, the judgmental and not so supportive people, the looks, and the many questions from anywhere and everywhere.

Everything became blurry; I didn't know how to pray anymore—what to even say to God at this point because in my mind, this was not supposed to be happening at all. We had waited for these miracles with anxiety and excitement and now all of this.

I liked to fix things and always figured out so many

aspects of my life with pen, paper and a vision. This one I couldn't. It was beyond me. The future just seemed so bleak. I didn't know if our children would enjoy a normal life ever. I wondered about them being stigmatized by society, friends and family.

I became very protective and felt the need to justify and explain my children and why they were the way they were if they acted out of character.

Emotional pain is one of the worst pains; you know it will be healed, but there is no timeline on when and you never know how; you just keep waiting. Sometimes you hope and other times you don't. You just wake up upset, angry and confused—all the bad emotions at once.

My prayer life at this point was on hold. I didn't know what to pray for or how to pray. I felt I had exhausted it all and I also felt God knew what was going on so what was the point.

I was totally lost!

Psalm 141:1-3

*I call to you, L*ORD*, come quickly to me;*
hear me when I call to you.
May my prayer be set before you like incense;
may the lifting up of my hands be like the evening
sacrifice
*Set a guard over my mouth, L*ORD*;*
keep watch over the door of my lips.

CHAPTER FOUR

ACCEPTANCE AND MANEUVER

It slowly started to sink in. I got up and started to make lemons out of this lemonade. I decided to read and join many social media groups so that I could learn a lot and get any resources that would help make life easier for our girls.

We looked out for early intervention school options, intensive speech therapy and applicable life skills tools. We took the girls for the school tests and enrolled them in the life skills program.

They would attend school for three hours then come home to speech therapy in the afternoons. I started to pay attention to details regarding what they liked and what they didn't like. They were both conscious of crowds and noise. They liked to line up their toys in a specific order. They had different sleeping patterns. Thankfully, they slept all night.

I now became more patient and understanding. I also engaged them a lot with the ABCs and 123s and learning toys that stimulate the brain.

I was numb at this point. I had accepted what was going on with our girls, living each day at a time. I started to look out for small milestones that I could hold on to, that could give me hope that there would be a turnaround.

I also felt the need to share this with those that were dear to me. I told my sisters, and even though they didn't understand the magnitude and I didn't go into much detail, they were very supportive. I did not tell my parents because I did not want them to worry from afar. I later explained the issue to my father and my mother witnessed it firsthand when she came to visit for the holidays. Rightfully, she was concerned. She prayed, and her prayers were very encouraging.

In the midst of all this, I was still pursuing my master's degree. Although it was a hectic period, the girls were always my motivation to complete the degree.

My sister Joyce was also living with us at the time, and for a couple of years, she took on the role of taking care of the girls wholeheartedly. She frequently took them to the park, and did strolls and walks with them in the malls. They were very fond of her. Alyssa was very attached to her and would co-sleep. She took care of their meals and daily routine. I was blessed to have her in my home during this time, as I was juggling a full-time and a part-time job. The good thing is I was done with school and had graduated—an achievement I was very excited about because I wanted to show my daughters that the sky is the limit.

My best friend and childhood friend, Sandra and her husband Emmanuel were very supportive right from when we were given the news and later the diagnosis. They often called to encourage and lift us up in prayer.

Their two beautiful children were in the same age range as my girls. They enjoyed playtime, sleepovers, hair braiding, and life being as normal as possible. They adapted to watching tv together; they all loved mickey mouse, Peppa Pig, Dora the Explorer, and many others. They started to learn the songs and it was amazing that while they were not able to construct sentences, they could sing these songs very well.

Life was now normal. The difficulties and challenges we were dealing with as a family were no longer in the forefront of our lives. The constant prayers, fasting and uplifting from people like my sister Charlotte, my parents, Emmanuel and Sandra, and my dear pastors were all I was clinging to at this point since I was personally struggling in this area.

Psalm 86:3-7

You are my God; have mercy on me, Lord,
for I call to you all day long.
Bring joy to your servant, Lord,
for I put my trust in you.
You, Lord, are forgiving and good,
abounding in love to all who call to you.
*Hear my prayer, L*ORD*;*
listen to my cry for mercy.
When I am in distress, I call to you,
because you answer me.

CHAPTER FIVE

ON MY KNEES

I felt a heavy heart each time I went to bed because my relationship with my God had become distant during this dark season in our lives. One Sunday while at church, it was announced there would be a meeting for the workers in the church and those who wanted to be workers in a fortnight. I made a mental note of it and decided I would attend since I was on the praise and worship team. I did not make much of it. I got back to my usual routine, but as time drew closer, I became interested in attending this meeting so I made up my mind to attend.

Saturday morning, I got dressed and went to the meeting. Our dear pastor spoke and the word, prayers, and fellowship impacted me in ways I could never imagine. I remember it was about serving God and being a worker on earth for God's people and kingdom. They laid hands on each one of us and prayed for us to have selfless hearts and serve God with wholeness, to be diligent, and the message covered that what you sow, so shall you reap. I got home and sat in my bathroom and wept, not because I was sad but because the revelation on this had opened my eyes. I did not pray; I talked a lot that evening to God and made up my mind I would work in the house of the Lord. I told God I would stay in the worship ministry since it was something I was already doing. I also decided I would join the children's ministry and sow into the children with the word. In turn, I hoped God would touch my children and heal them.

Sunday, I went to church and before the service began, I was called into the office by my pastor who asked if I would be interested in taking charge of the children. This was a big confirmation for me, considering that I had just talked to God the previous night while on my bathroom floor.

I went back home, sat down, and thought of ways I could add value to these children. I drew up schedules and discussed the best way to teach the children with the other teachers. This was the beginning of my journey to get back on track with the relationship I had with my God. I taught the children's ministry and also was in the praise and worship team. With my focus on these things, slowly, my stress was replaced with peace; my anxiety with joy and my tears with happiness. I no longer saw my children and their issues. In fact, interacting with the children I taught allowed me to see that each parent had a struggle of their own. It may not have been the same as ours, but it still was something that kept some awake at night. I became more engrossed in working and did it even when I was tired and when I wavered because I knew one day, God would hear my prayers, see my sacrifice, and heal my children.

I continued to seek God and this time, it was different. I was no longer angry. I didn't have questions anymore and I had made peace with whatever God had decided. I knew then that even if my children didn't get healed, God would still make it possible for us to take care of them fully as He was the one that had given them to us.

Psalm 20:6-9

Now, this I know:
The LORD gives victory to his anointed.
He answers him from his heavenly sanctuary
with the victorious power of his right hand.
Some trust in chariots and some in horses,
but we trust in the name of the LORD our God.
They are brought to their knees and fall,
but we rise up and stand firm.
LORD, give victory to the king!
Answer us when we call!

CHAPTER SIX

TRUSTING GOD

Singing No one like you, Jesus by Eben in this chapter.

The girls at this point had joined an elementary school and were in special education classes. We got daily and weekly progress reports and had meetings with the teachers and therapists who were assisting with their learning.

My personal journey and relationship with God continued to grow. Every milestone with the girls was noticed and celebrated as a family. During this time I learned about the importance of fasting, sowing seeds, and giving tithe and offering. I explored the word of God more and more and started to understand Him in ways I never did before because of this season we were in.

My trust in God and His process started to grow. I always relied on scripture and verses like, *His plans are to prosper and not to harm us.* Around that time, I was also giving God praise for allowing me to finish my master's degree. Also, I had finally been offered a job, even after the gap in my employment that had deterred employers from hiring me in the past. We also decided to purchase our first home, and through it all, I saw God; I saw destiny helpers sent by Him, and His favor and abundance surrounded us.

Seeing God move in other areas of our lives made me realize that God had not abandoned us as I had felt before. I started to relate to the God of love, mercy, and understanding and decided to trust His ways.

Charlotte's way of living was also very encouraging to me on this journey of trusting God. Her prayerful lifestyle, despite the challenges she would go through each time, was very inspiring. I looked forward to fasting and praying with her. Her challenges sometimes caught me off guard, but her faith was so amazing and I wanted that kind of trust in God.

My relationship and walk with God improved tremendously and my trust in Him was in a much better place. I still had questions and every now and then, the devil would make me pity myself and the children.

During this time, I also got a word of knowledge from my sister and my pastor about God wanting to bless us with a son. This was the moment where my trust and faith were put to a total test. All my fears of this happening all over again came back and I said no. I was not going to even try, lest we end up with a child with the same issues. I then had a dream and this was the confirmation that God wanted me to walk in obedience and trust Him. I will not lie; this was so hard for me. I was okay with how things were, just the two beautiful girls God had blessed us with. I decided to take a leap of faith and go to my pastor's office. I knelt and asked her to pray for me. I was overcome by peace and that's when I knew this was a blessing. Before I knew it, I was pregnant, the nine months were fine. I had the usual pregnancy issues, nothing serious. We welcomed our son in August. I am glad I walked in faith, trusted God, and that He blessed us with another beautiful gift.

Psalm 77:14
You are the God who performs miracles;
you display your power among the peoples.

CHAPTER SEVEN

THE MIRACLES

Welcoming our third child was overwhelming. I was excited but nervous at the same time because I had all these questions and thoughts running through my mind. What if he/she would be like our older two children or even worse? I remember I was a basketcase one day, so I prayed to God. I got a surprise call from my sister who told me that the Lord had said not to worry and that everything was going to be okay. She also added it was a boy as confirmation. Words can't describe the emotions I had, but I was so comforted by the Lord's words. The following week, I had to go for a checkup that involved blood work and the results came out the next day, including the—gender and indeed it was a boy.

At the time, God's goodness had already started manifesting, but I was consumed with worry that I did not stop to take it all in. My workplace had introduced a new insurance policy and everything about it favored me. People were excited that finally after so many years, we had the chance to have good health insurance. While I was still marveling at the news, it was announced that our supervisor was being changed and we would be working with someone from out of state. Things were changing quickly, and I was concerned about the flexibility to schedule my checkups since the current supervisor understood me and worked in the same office as I did.

Later, we each got to have a one on one with the new supervisor and she was really nice. After about six weeks, she called me into a meeting and told me she was going to let me go work from home based on my metrics and performance, and also because I was pregnant. She also stated that the rest of the team would transition slowly to work from home as well. Look at God!

It was a miracle and good news came one after the other. My ears couldn't believe this; I was going to work from home which meant no more worries about the children and work at the same time. The changes did not happen immediately. I started working from home in my third trimester. My mother was also able to come and help me with the children when my due date was approaching. This was truly amazing.

During this time, I got to focus on the good, and the girls' struggles were also beginning to lessen. Our older child Crystal was now more independent, was totally out of diapers and could now understand and follow instructions. Her sister Alyssa was still struggling, but she always helped her with the light chores.

We welcomed Nathaniel during hurricane Harvey. The storm was horrible. It had affected hospitals and the floods were devastating. I got a call that all surgeries that were not emergencies had been postponed and that all hospitals in the area were closed except for the one where I was supposed to give birth. God took care of it all and everything went well.

Psalm 34:1-3

*I will bless the L<small>ORD</small> at all times:His praise shall
continually be in my mouth.
My soul shall make her boast in the L<small>ORD</small>: the hum-
ble shall hear thereof, and be glad.
O magnify the L<small>ORD</small> with me, and let us exalt his
name together.*

CHAPTER EIGHT

THANKSGIVING

My mother stayed for two months helping with the children. It was such a blessing not having to worry about the older children. I could now focus on the newborn. My thoughts totally shifted as I concentrated on getting better. At that point, we had celebrated a few milestones including the older child, Crystal finally being out of diapers. She was now fully expressing herself and helping around the house, all excited to be a big sister. She liked being involved in taking care of her baby brother. Her personality started to really become noticeable. From a young, timid, nonverbal child to now expressing herself really well. Blessed with a loving heart, she was a constant advocate for everyone in the home.

Alyssa, on the other hand, was still struggling with instruction and diapers, but seeing the transformation with Crystal made me know that God was doing a great work and answering prayers. I stopped praying and started praising. It was always a moment of thanks when I saw that a new milestone was achieved.

My father-in-law also came and stayed with us for six months. Words can't even begin to describe how humbled I was. He took care of Nathaniel from day one. At the time, I had gone back to work full time, and the girls were enrolled in school, so the work had lessened. I did not have to worry at all, as he was always by his side. We settled into a simple daily routine. Every moment I observed my family and God's goodness, I could not help but marvel. Sometimes, those thoughts of delays crept in but I stayed hopeful. When Nathaniel was about nine months old, my father-in-law left. He had done such an amazing job with him. I remember my pastor telling me how God had taken care of my worries about who would help with taking care of him by sending our parents. When she said it, I remembered my sister telling me while I was pregnant, not to worry and that God would take care of everything.

In no time, Nathaniel was celebrating his first

birthday with his cousin Jaycee. He developed issues with his skin, had severe eczema and also had issues with eating solids but never did I lose sleep, even for a day, because I had seen the girls who struggled with way worse become healed. I knew that in due time and in His season, the God we serve would take all that away too. What shall I render to Jehovah? For He has done so very much for me. I am humbled as I write this beautiful chapter.

Psalm 40:3
He put a new song in my mouth,
a hymn of praise to our God.
*Many will see and fear the L*ORD
and put their trust in Him.

CHAPTER NINE

BEAUTIFUL BEGINNINGS

The testimonies in this chapter not only show God's love and mercy but His promise never to leave me nor forsake me and my family. The girls each stopped wearing diapers after a very long time, and we celebrated that great milestone with praises and thanks to God.

Crystal started to not only do extremely well in school but also take charge and lead both at school and at home. She was getting all A's in every subject and was reading very well with no help, for which she had been given class awards. She also showed interest in extra curricular activities like any other child—with a love for swimming and outdoor sports. For school, they decided to let her join mainstream classes for science and social studies once a week to adapt. Previously, she had been a child that was either not talking or crying all the time for everything and anything. She was also sensitive to noises and crowds, but now, her true self was emerging. We started to see that she has a very big heart, and is extremely kind and caring. She also started to do her chores even without being told. Her personality started to really shine and she was no longer the shy, timid girl. Instead, she is the life of the party, very bubbly and in charge in environments she deems safe. She asks a lot of questions and argues all too well. We call her our little lawyer and she calls herself 'the little dentist' since that is what she hopes to be when she grows up.

Alyssa, our very free-spirited child, has grown to have her own uniqueness. She is reserved yet passionate and specific about the few things she loves. She looks up to her big sister for direction. She is very organized and careful with her things. She is obsessed with her tablet, sometimes watching videos in other languages, which amazes us. She has a very independent mind. She still struggles with certain directions; however, we work around those concerns by using colors to describe objects. Her sister sometimes calls her a princess and other times, a policeman, because of her tough side which comes out every now and then when she needs to use it.

Both girls are smart. They pay attention to detail in ways you could never imagine for their ages and milestones. For instance, Crystal has a very good photographic memory when it comes to places. She only needs to go to them once for her to remember exactly where and how to get there.

People that meet and interact with them now, never having known them before are astounded at the history and the complete turnaround. I know it was the Lord's doing and it was marvelous in our sight.

For families that have a loved one on the autism spectrum, there is hope. The bible says in Psalm 42:11 "Why art thou cast down, O my soul? and why art thou disquieted within me? hope thou in God: for I shall yet praise Him, who is the health of my countenance, and my God." The God that delivered our children will do the same for you if you have faith and believe.

Be blessed.

www.ingramcontent.com/pod-product-compliance
Lightning Source LLC
Chambersburg PA
CBHW061159040426
42445CB00013B/1743